Claudia Tomlinson

SEVEN SURVIVAL STEPS
for Black and Minority Ethnic Staff Working in the National Health Service

Seven
Survival
Steps

for Black and Minority Ethnic Staff Working in the National Health Service

Claudia Tomlinson

Copyright © 2017 Claudia Tomlinson

All rights reserved.

Dedication:

This book is dedicated to all the passionate, hardworking NHS staff and leaders who strive and struggle for fairness and equality, and who provide care and treatment to the nation.

Contents

Acknowledgements

Thank you to the following who have provided inspiration and guidance:

Alex Raikes and SARI

Niema Burns

Dr Umesh Prabhu

Mrs Michelle Simmons-Safo

What people are saying about this book:

"*Thank you so much for writing a survival guide for Black NHS Staff. When I found your articles last year, it put my experiences of last 10yrs in perspective!*"

"*It gave me confidence to speak up and an impetus to do something.*"

"*I frequently resonate on the Seven Survival Steps for Black and Minority (BME) NHS Staff and highly recommend it to others in order to confidently navigate around the organisation*"

"*It is refreshing to read and understand that there is a need to change and celebrate the contribution that BME staff can make to the modern NHS.*"

Introduction

What does the term BME mean? Once, it was well known and understood, now it is more usual to hear people say "what does BME mean?" than for them to signal understanding and not need an explanation. This situation could be interpreted positively, that we are now in a post-racial era in Britain and people don't need to know the abbreviation for Black and Minority Ethnic people and communities. It could signal that no one any longer sees colour, ethnicity, or racial diversity.

With the proliferation of race equality legislation, increasingly diverse British cities, and the growth of the numbers of BME staff in the public sector workforce we have been seduced into accepting the idea of a post-racial, and indeed a post-racial society. Also, as the history of BME immigration to the UK, on a large scale, has progressed through the decades and there are now four or five generations in the UK. That has been seen as sufficient time for early problems of the 1950s through to the 1990s to be ironed out.

There are many public attitudes surveys to suggest that there is greater 'tolerance' towards BME people in the UK, and indeed the British Monarchy may be poised to welcome its first BME member by marriage.

Instead, many are concerned that there has been a rolling back of sympathetic political and public concern about the welfare of BME immigrants. The appetite for empathy has receded. There is a new narrative about putting the British first. Equality for BME people has come to be viewed with suspicion, disdain, bitterness, anger and hostility. The fear is that if BME people are treated equally, and have equal opportunities, that mean some non-BME people will do less well than BME people. Have a smaller cut of the cake. The debates that recognise the situation of BME immigrants to the UK have been muted or even silenced. This has resulted in the peril that many BME people still find themselves in, being ignored.

Politicians from all parties have colluded with this narrative, and it has been part of the conversations that have funnelled people to the ballot boxes to put their crosses for candidates who seem to promise to turn the clock back to a more homogenous past. This is not a political book, and politics can only ever be part of the solution. But no one should ever forget or ignore the power of politics.

Being BME is about skin colour, migration history, culture. It is always a story of a seeking, questing, hoping and striving. Dreaming of a better tomorrow for ourselves. It is not an easy decision to shed culture, family and friends and country for a promise of a job. These are decisions that change family trees and destinies for generations.

NHS Workforce Race Equality

The NHS staff survey programme was introduced in 2006 to formally measure staff experience on a range of indicators annually. The results each year have mirrored social inequalities in race and ethnicity. The annual national staff survey programme has demonstrated consistently higher reported levels of bullying, harassment, and discrimination in BME staff, than non-BME staff. Multiple data sources exist to demonstrate a poorer experience for BME staff working in the NHS including the following:

- Access to training and development opportunities
- Poor promotion prospect with a low 'glass ceiling'
- Bullying and harassment
- Race discrimination
- Over representation in disciplinary proceedings

Working in the NHS is a popular career choice for people from BME backgrounds in the UK, and they are a very valuable resource to organisations, and wider society. The historical context of the recruitment of BME workers from former British colonies to make up the shortfall in the workforce required for the newly formed NHS have been well documented. In summary, the expectation on British politicians and society was that these would be workers who would fill unskilled and semi-skilled positions in the NHS, as a short term policy measure, and that would be the extent of their participation in the NHS and wider society. They would fill this gap, created by the expansion of the welfare state, and labour shortage following the end of the Second World War.

They would then go home, leaving British society and culture unchanged. As they were migrating to work at a specific social stratum, there would be no question of a claim to equality, they were here to work at the lower levels of the economy, and after the British workforce was sufficiently re-built and developed to the level of self-sufficiency, the immigrants would then go home.

Many of the migrants chose to remain and make Britain their permanent homes due to the levels of underdevelopment and poverty in their post-colonial home countries. There was also continued demand for their labour to meet the needs of the growing population, and the new welfare state. Britain has never achieved self-sufficiency in providing a workforce for the NHS. There has continued to be a programme of overseas recruitment from countries around the world, including some of the poorest countries. The new black and Asian migrants started to send for the children they had left behind in their homeland, and put them in British schools. They started to settle, buying homes in the UK, and became an established in homes and communities. Some branched out from the NHS and moved to work in other areas of the economy, or start businesses. The idea that they would forfeit a career and regular income to return to an unstable post-colonial economy and lifestyle proved to be an erroneous belief and plan.

Returning to their homeland, at least in the short to medium term, was therefore postponed or put on ice completely. Some then started to plan that their return home would be something they would achieve after retirement. Many began sending money to relatives back home, and to begin the process of building their homes back in their country of origin, which would then be ready for them to return to when they retired.

Things changed for everyone. For the migrants, they were now here for the long haul. That meant instead of a two, three or five-year career, the migrants were now planning for a lifelong career in the NHS, of thirty more years at least. They would now not be working jobs, but developing careers, alongside everyone else in the country.

This change remained an unspoken narrative. But two sets of expectations started to develop and moved along two different tracks. As the migrants had now made Britain their permanent home, they would strive and want to achieve and experience fulfilled careers.

The NHS maintained the original narrative and trajectory of viewing and treating the migrants, as low skilled, low paid workforce, here to provide and serve those in British society, mirroring their service (through slavery, indenture contracts, and low paid work service work) in the colonial countries they left behind.

To address some of these inequalities, NHS England introduced the Workforce Race Equality Standard (WRES) , in 2015, and established a national implementation team to oversee this programme. WRES has raised the profiles of the issues and required most NHS organisations to report data for each indicator.

NHS Workforce Race Equality Standard Indicators (Comparative Data for BME compared with White Staff)	
1.	Percentage of staff in each of the AfC Bands 1-9 and VSM (including executive Board members) compared with the percentage of staff in the overall workforce
2.	Relative likelihood of staff being appointed from shortlisting across all posts
3.	Relative likelihood of staff entering the formal disciplinary process, as measured by entry into a formal disciplinary investigation
4.	Relative likelihood of staff accessing non-mandatory training and CPD 5. KF 25.
5.	Percentage of staff experiencing harassment, bullying or abuse from patients, relatives or the public in last 12 months
6.	Percentage of staff experiencing harassment, bullying or abuse from staff in last 12 months
7.	Percentage believing that trust provides equal opportunities for career progression or promotion
8.	In the last 12 months have you personally experienced discrimination at work from any of the following? b) Manager/ team leader or other colleagues Board representation indicator
9.	Percentage difference between the organisations' Board voting membership and its overall workforce

WRES indicators provide an additional driver for innovation and action within NHS organisations, however grassroots action and innovation is a gap that needs to be addressed to achieve significant and enduring change.

Legacy

There is value in referencing historical, colonial relationships stretching back many years as this culture is felt by many to be a dynamic very much at play in modern race relations, that has withstood the passage of hundreds of years.

With second, third and fourth generations of the children of immigrants being born and settling into British society, and laying claim to equality with the non-BME Britons, tensions are close to the surface because of unresolved expectations, embedded historical beliefs, and cultural norms.

The experience of immigrants working in the NHS, that of discrimination, can lead to limited future expectations of success and progress. To survive, people sometimes choose to remain in the safe spaces they create or identify. Safety is those spaces where they are least challenged, in other words those spaces that are designated as where they belong. So people can sometimes develop a mentality where it is safer to remain in the lower grades, in menial jobs, as then they meet expectations, and do not generate an uncomfortable narrative for non-BME people who struggle to see them differently. These beliefs and attitudes can linger, and pass down the generations, and can partly explain the choices made by some BME staff about the roles they pursue. These are the only roles they see as being open to them.

These are the beliefs that as BME workers, we labour for non-BME people who set the standards and terms by which we provide our labour. We do back-breaking work, undesirable, uncomfortable work that the host population doesn't want to do. We do it because that is our 'lot' in life. To do hard, physical graft. That is our raison d'etre on earth. Because others have demanded, forced, organised us into that situation to such an extent that for some people, it is an ingrained self-expectation.

This historical context is important to confront in this debate as it is the elephant in the room, a massive elephant that prevents focus on anything else. So this must be part of the debate, an uncomfortable debate, but it is a critical starting point.

It is this historical context that leads to the conferring of less favourable benefits and poorer treatment of BME staff in the NHS because that was the original contact, and a new contract has not been agreed. The old contract stated, in simple terms, BME staff, you can come here, work for us, where we tell you, when we tell you and for the conditions we prescribe and accept your lot. The new contract states 'we expect of you what we were told to expect when you first came, now you say you want equality with us, which is not how we see you. And who will fill the gap if you become like us? Who will do the work we invited you over here to do if you progress, we don't want to do those terrible jobs, we don't want you jumping over us, so you need to keep doing it. Sorry. Someone has to be at the bottom of the pile, this is our country, we are privileged to own this nation, and to have once owned you, and we will still behave as if we own you'.

It is unpalatable for some non-BME British people to be without resources such as money, homes or jobs when there are BME people with these resources in Britain, derived through their own hard labour and efforts. There can be resentment that non-BME people are in homes and jobs while non-BME British are unemployed, and without the standard of housing they desire, or who are, homeless. This is not what non-BME people thought would happen. The thinking in some quarters can be that Britain is a country for Non-BME people, and they are entitled to the best it has to offer, they must come before anyone else, before all 'outsiders'. This is the same narrative that is present in the NHS, and mirrors what is happening in wider society. The best of the NHS, must be available for non-BME staff and patients, and what is unwanted, can be picked up by migrants, or 'outsiders'.

Whilst this book does not provide political analysis of race and discrimination, politicians, of all parties, have exploited social division for political gain over the past fifty years. They swing between protecting the rights of racial minorities, to silence or hostility to the presence of immigrants in the UK.

At many points in one's career, there is a need to manage low-level or micro-aggressions as a result of race-based discrimination and prejudice. Examples of low level micro-agressions are those that are barely perceptible to the naked eye. Two nurses at the nurses bay, one BME and the other non-BME, with the BME one being the one nearest those arriving for help. Visitors, including other NHS staff working for the same organisation go to the non-BME nurse to speak to rather than the BME nurse. This is particularly problematic if the BME nurse is the senior and the non-BME nurse much more junior and then has to refer the person making the inquiry to the BME nurse. Similarly, BME and non-BME staff being spoken to by a non-BME person notices that they very rarely get any eye contact which all goes to the non-BME participants in the conversation.

Lawrence and Keleher's excellent 2004 paper on structural racism is one of the best accounts of how societal racism works to disadvantage and advantage BME and non-BME people. People from all backgrounds are recommended to read and review this paper to educate and inform. Their analysis was developed in America and is referenced on the United States history, social structures, but has much wider, international application. The define structural racism in the following way:

Structural Racism lies underneath, all around and across society. It encompasses:

(1) History, which lies underneath the surface, providing the foundation for white supremacy in this country.

(2) Culture, which exists all around our everyday lives, providing the normalization and replication of racism and,

(3) Interconnected institutions and policies, they key relationships and rules across society providing the legitimacy and reinforcements to maintain and perpetuate racism (Lawrence and Keleher, 2004).

There is now more attention on experience of those who use public services, and this has provided added impetus to the question of staff experience. In 2014, the publication of a seminal piece of research by Roger Kline at Middlesex University Business School "The Snowy White Peaks of the NHS" described the background and context of the experience of BME staff in the NHS, and how patient safety and experience is affected by a very damaging situation.

If you are from a black and minority ethnic (BME) background, and work in the NHS in the UK, you will already know that survival can be the name of the game. As well as doing the day job, whether you are a consultant, a hospital porter, a chief executive, a nurse or an administrator there are factors you are far more likely to have to negotiate than your non-BME colleagues.

Why this book?

This book was written originally as a series of articles for the Huffington Post UK, where I am on their panel of bloggers. I chose to write this book as a mechanism for self-support and development at a time when I was experiencing the biggest challenge of my professional career. I went through a steep learning curve, and in fact found that my learning wasn't new, but a harnessing and scaffolding of years of knowledge, observation, action and experience. I outline my learning and the journey I went through, at the outset of the book. This book is for anyone interested in learning more about the experience of BME staff in the NHS, and for staff wanting to address barriers they may face. It is primarily for staff that are passionate about their careers and want to ensure a fair, positive and successful experience whilst working in the NHS.

Survival Step One

Line up your defence

Today's preparation determines
tomorrow's achievement

(ANON)

Developing a line of defence is recommended as the first step because if you are from a BME background, and working in the NHS, you are statistically more likely to face disciplinary action, bullying, harassment and discrimination. Three recommendations are made under this step of things you need to have in place from the first day of your NHS career. The three actions you are recommended to have in place are trade union membership, insurance cover, and organised personal finances.

There are many platitudes about the value of pre-paredness, and most have at least a kernel of truth. Knowing that one is prepared, provides freedom to enjoy peace that comes from knowing that a plan is in place if the worst happens. For BME staff, the worst is more likely to happen than for non-BME staff.

Trade Union and Professional Body Membership

NHS staff sometimes query the value of trade union membership, particularly when having to find sub-scription funds out of a limited pay packet Further, In the face of the erosion of some of the powers of trade unions it has become increasingly common to find discourses questioning the benefits of trade union membership. Trade unions are membership organisations working to obtain the best workplace terms and conditions for their members. They charge a membership subscription in return for a range of membership benefits. Typical membership benefits across most health unions include:

- Contract checking
- Employment advice
- Personal injury.
- Criminal Injuries
- Work-related criminal offences
- Wills
- Counselling

- Legal services
- Conveyancing
- Clinical negligence
- Free legal advice
- Learning and development
- Access to health and academic journals

Membership	Trade Union
Dieticians, Dietetic Support Workers, Students	British Dietetic Association
Doctors of all grades in hospital and GP practice, and students.	British Medical Association
A general membership, representing ambulance staff, domestics, maintenance, support and professional staff.	GMB
Represents health and social care staff from most professional disciplines and NHS job roles.	Unison

Membership	Trade Union
A general membership, representing Allied Health Professional, maintenance and domestic staff, and a range of professional health staff.	Unite
Midwives	Royal College of Midwives
Qualified nurses, and non-qualified nursing support workers	Royal College of Nursing

The reality is that when staff run into employment difficulties at work in the NHS, the absence of trade union membership benefits is often sorely felt.

This step is being recommended here for BME NHS staff to have in place from the first day they start working for the NHS as an employee, whether in training, part or full time, and whatever field you work in, and to maintain it throughout your career.

There are trade unions covering every type of work in the NHS but some of the main ones are Unison, Unite, the British Medical Association, The Royal College of Nursing, The Royal College of Midwives, and GMB. Some of these act as professional bodies for registered and qualified staff, as well as including unions that any NHS worker can join.

There are different levels of possible involvement and different benefits are achieved with each level of involvement. As a member, unions provide you with from advice, support and information from their union representatives and branch staff. As a union representative, you will assist and represent members. This level of involvement bring additional benefits to you as you gain increased awareness of how organisations work, policies, pressures and planning. It can also bring protections in that the organisation is restricted in the degree to which they can discipline a representative, they must consult the union before acting against a representative or official.

Insurance

Professional Indemnity insurance provides you with cover in the event that you are successfully sued by people who have received your services, who feel they have been harmed or injured as a result. Before taking this out as a separate insurance, check that it is not included in any union or professional body membership you already have in place. If you are employed, your employer is liable for any clinical negligence claim brought in relation to or independent basis, you should ensure clinical negligence cover is in place.

Legal Services Insurance may be needed to cover to pay for the costs of legal services to bring a legal action. This may be included in your union membership, and will pay for the cost of making a claim in the event of an employment dispute. Which has produced a good guide about choosing **legal expenses insurance**, but quotes are available from comparison websites. Home contents insurance often includes legal services insurance so it is worth checking whether you already have it. If you do not have insurance in place, but need to bring a claim, and cannot cover legal costs yourself, speak with the Citizens Advice Bureau, and discuss with your solicitor special forms of insurance called Before the Event, and After the Event Insurance.

Other insurance to be considered are income protection insurance, and mortgage protection, but first look the life insurance benefits in your employment pension scheme, particularly if you are in the NHS pension scheme, which is highly recommended.

With all insurance schemes, they can provide false reassurance because it will always be up to the insurance companies whether they will pay your claim.

To ensure absolute confidence that you will be able to rely on legal services, you can only do so by putting a legal fund aside yourself. Through astute financial management, you can build up an emergency fund specifically to meet some legal services that you might need to bring. The capacity to pay for a few hours of legal advice/action can be sufficient to deliver good outcomes. Do your research; and speak to a few law firms.

Personal Finances

Effective control and management of your personal finances is possibly the most important line of defence, and this will need to be in place if you are to ensure the ability to continuously and comfortably pay subscriptions for insurance, union membership etc. There are many personal finance resources and experts, and much of the advice is available in books, websites, blogs, podcasts, and vlogs. Good ones are ones are **Money Saving Expert** and the **Money Advice Service**. The single most important advice that is almost universally agreed is the need to have an emergency fund, often described as a financial cushion, or rainy day fund. This is a sum of money that is set aside, in an easy access account, sufficient to cover your expenses for a period of time should an unexpected emergency happen. In the context of this discussion, the sum would need to be sufficient to cover your expenses for a period during which you are not working. The minimum recommended varies, but ultimately your personal circumstances will need to determine how much you need to set aside. Readers are recommended to obtain impartial, independent advice to guide your own decisions on your insurance and financial needs.

Survival Step Two

Write a new script committing to higher levels of engagement

Every great dream begins with a dreamer. Always remember, you have within you the strength, the patience, and the passion to reach for the stars to change the world.

HARRIET TUBMAN

Survival Step 2 is about developing a new mindset and telling a new narrative about the type of contribution black and ethnic minority staff can make to a modern NHS.

BME NHS staff today face a bigger challenge which is to confront limited and self-limiting attitudes and expectations in themselves. Too many BME NHS staff bolster and reinforce these attitudes and expectations of themselves. For example, each time a BME NHS worker declines to apply for a senior position because they feel they will not be successful, and that a non-BME NHS worker is more likely to get it, they are bolstering expectations and self-expectations. Self-belief and a sense of equal entitlement is a must for success for BME staff in the NHS.

The step that BME workers are recommended to take at Survival Step two is to commit to a higher level of engagement at an early stage in their NHS career, whatever their role or job. This means moving away from the self-belief that doing a job is solely about doing hard labour, no more, no less. There's nothing wrong with hard graft, but why leave it at that?

Writing a new narrative

To write a new narrative for yourself there is a simple exercise using the Narrative Projection Technique. This is a personal tool for you to use to plot out where you want to be in fifteen years. If you are now a Band 6 Junior Charge Nurse or sister and want to be CEO or Director of Nursing in ten years' time, you need to have a crystal clear goal-oriented plan for every step on your journey. It is true that luck and fate can play a part in promotion, such as someone unexpectedly leaving a post, or retiring giving rise to a vacancy. You would still need to have done years of ground-work to ensure you are in a position to get that job. Despite the fact that there are so many BME staff in the NHS, most are too far away from the senior ranks to be able to apply for Trust Board vacancies when they arise.

You can use this Narrative Projection Tool to build a personal narrative, the story you are going to tell about how you made it to the role.

Narrative Projection Tool – 0 to Fifteen Years

	1 Year	2 Year	5 Years	7 Years	10 Years	15 Years
Promotions applied for	0	2				
Highest Grade	Band 5	Band 6	Band 8A	Band 8C	Assistant Director	Executive Director
Highest Qualification	Diploma	Degree	-	-		
Additional roles held	0	1 (Union Equality Rep)				
Awards received	0	1 (Staff Excellence Monthly award)				
Conference poster presentations	0	1 (RCN Conference)				
Conferences spoken at	0	1 (Allied Health Professionals Conference)				

As a BME NHS worker you will need to use the same systems and channels to get to the top that are available to everyone. Participate fully in appraisals, undertake training and personal development. But when the system isn't working for you, that's when you will need to take steps and decisions to achieve your goal.

Changing to a better job environment

People remain in particular jobs for many reasons other than experiencing fulfillment in a specific role. Staff members are happy to remain in the same organisation, or sometimes even in the same department, if possible, for the entirety of their career. Factors that keep people in a specific role are that it is complex, skilled job that will retain their interest and development needs for a long time. Additionally people remain in jobs because it is close to home, part of their local community and identity, they have formed close relationships and friendships where they work and it suits their family needs. If a staff member needs a job that is stable, fits in with their family life and they can travel to and from work easily, and the people are nice, then for some staff there will be no circumstances where they will apply for another job.

However, if these factors don't prevent staff from leaving, I strongly advocate that staff leave their job for a better job or work environment in order to progress. Care will need to be taken to ensure a solid job offer is in place if you need to go straight to another job.

With your personal finance plans in place, you should always be in a position to survive for three to six months without a job, should the circumstances arrive. So if you prefer to take a short break from work, and are not too risk averse, you can choose to take a break from work altogether to reflect on your options.

Stop doing jobs start delivering roles

Changing job regularly is critical for career success, and you will need to be changing jobs every twelve to twenty four months in order to successfully progress. Move towards thinking in terms of roles rather than jobs. A role is a part you are playing, developing growing and delivering, for a period of time as opposed to a job which has a sense of routine, static, drudgery, and uninspiring activity. Stop doing jobs, start delivering roles instead. This came alive for me when I worked as a contract consultant/manager for a period of two years. During that time, I learned to package and market myself according to my skills on my CV which made me see myself very differently after years of doing jobs. I learnt what the high demand skills were, such as Prince 2, and paid for myself to undertake the course, and I became highly in demand as a project manager thereafter.

You can determine what role you want to be doing, and market yourself as such. When I became very interested in becoming a commissioner I was working as a team manager in a community mental health service, and carried a caseload of community patients. Approximately one year after I decided to become a commissioner, I left my job as a community team manager and became a Strategic Commissioning Manager. As part of my preparation, I was in regular contact with commissioners, and made a point of observing exactly what they did, how they worked, the language they used, the organisational culture and values. I also did a lot of reading, and studied many job descriptions for commissioners to identify they type of job I might be interested in. I studied the Person Specifications and even though on the surface, the jobs of Team Manager and Strategic Commissioning Manager required interchangeable skillset. In fact I soon realised I was in a very strong position as not many commissioners had the extensive experience of delivering services. The other competencies such as monitoring progress, writing reports, and feeding back at meetings were part of my role as Team Manager.

I made the decision to package my offer at the interview as something the recruiter would feel they were missing out on if they did not appoint me.

Role Evaluation Tool

When you start a new job you should have in place a system for evaluating the value of the role in terms of your long term trajectory. You should be able to form a view within the first month, or even first week of the likely value of the role for delivering the benefits you hoped for. However it is good to systematically evaluate the role as you go along and using something along the lines of the Role Evaluation Tool may assist you. Staff often think in terms of experience when seeking to build a career, and that is important. However, experience may prove to be less important than a set of transferable skills. There is are a set of core skills that you need to master, and demonstrate at interviews and in work roles that are critical for progress. These are communication, technical skills (the skills needed to deliver the specific role such as catering), presentation, IT, leadership and planning skills. The best leaders excel in these competencies, and these are what you should be aiming at enhancing in each work role. To use the Role Evaluation Tool, simply track your progress on each of the core skills in each job, scoring out of ten at different points through time. So if when you first start you find there are average opportunities for building your communication skills, you would score this 5 out of ten with ten being the highest possible score. If after 24 months, you find the opportunities grew since you first started, but have since receded, you will be able to form an overall view of the value of the role.

Role Evaluation Tool						
Core Skills	3 months	6 months	12 months	18 months	24 months	
		Opportunity and practice				
Communication skills	5/10	4/10	7/10	6/10	4/10	
Technical skills	4/10	5/5	6/10	6/10	4/10	
Presentation/ teaching/coaching						
IT Skills						
Leadership						
Organisational and planning skills						

Conscious Time Out

If you choose to consciously take some time out from work, during this time, you can complete short courses to improve your employability. This gives you the added flexibility of undertaking courses that you choose and see them as relevant to further your ambitious dreams, rather than the modest expectations of an appraisal document. BME staff often feel they are less likely to be funded and released from their work duties to undertake a Master's Degree, for example.

I argue that if you want your Master's Degree, ask for it at appraisal, and if it is not granted, ask for a formal review by a senior manager to establish the justification of why you have not been permitted to do the course. If there are examples of other staff who have been funded and supported to do the course, there would need to be a clear justification why you have been denied it.

So, committing to higher levels of engagement and writing a new narrative is about taking bold action to move out of the lane you feel you are trapped in. Any BME worker can do this.

For example, if you are a hospital cleaner, take an interest in NHS Cleaning Standards, join in hospital wide cleaning audits, patient experience projects on hospital cleanliness and patient safety initiatives. Read about cleaning, write about cleaning. Get prepared because, even though cleaning is critical to patient care and safety, you might want to do more than the actual mopping one day. From my observations, most hospital cleaners are black and ethnic minority, particularly in inner city areas, with the cleaning and Facilities Manager or Supervisors, and Directors of Estates and Facilities are mostly non-BME.

If you work in the caring professions, or are a technician or scientist the same tenet applies to you. Do the hard labour bit really well, but at the same time, commit to a higher level of engagement. To commit to engage at a higher level, these are the steps you are recommended to do for yourself:

a) Government and politics - find out about the Government, the Opposition and their policies for the NHS. Learn about local politics - who's in charge locally and what are their policies, who are the local councillors, the MPs, their interests, and how do they engage with your organisation?

b) Read the Five Year Forward View - this is the agreed national plan for the NHS until 2020. You must talk about this at every interview you go to, whatever job and whatever level you work at in the NHS.

c) Become familiar with the NHS Workforce Race Equality Standard - new standards for race equality introduced into the NHS in 2015

d) Read the Health Services Journal regularly - ask your NHS librarian for online access

e) Participate in Social Media, just reading content as a minimum - Twitter, and Facebook are key for networking, and for fast sharing of news, information, debates and discussion

f) Websites to follow: Care Quality Commission, NHS Trust Development Authority, Monitor, and NHS England.

g) Read the quality national and local papers.

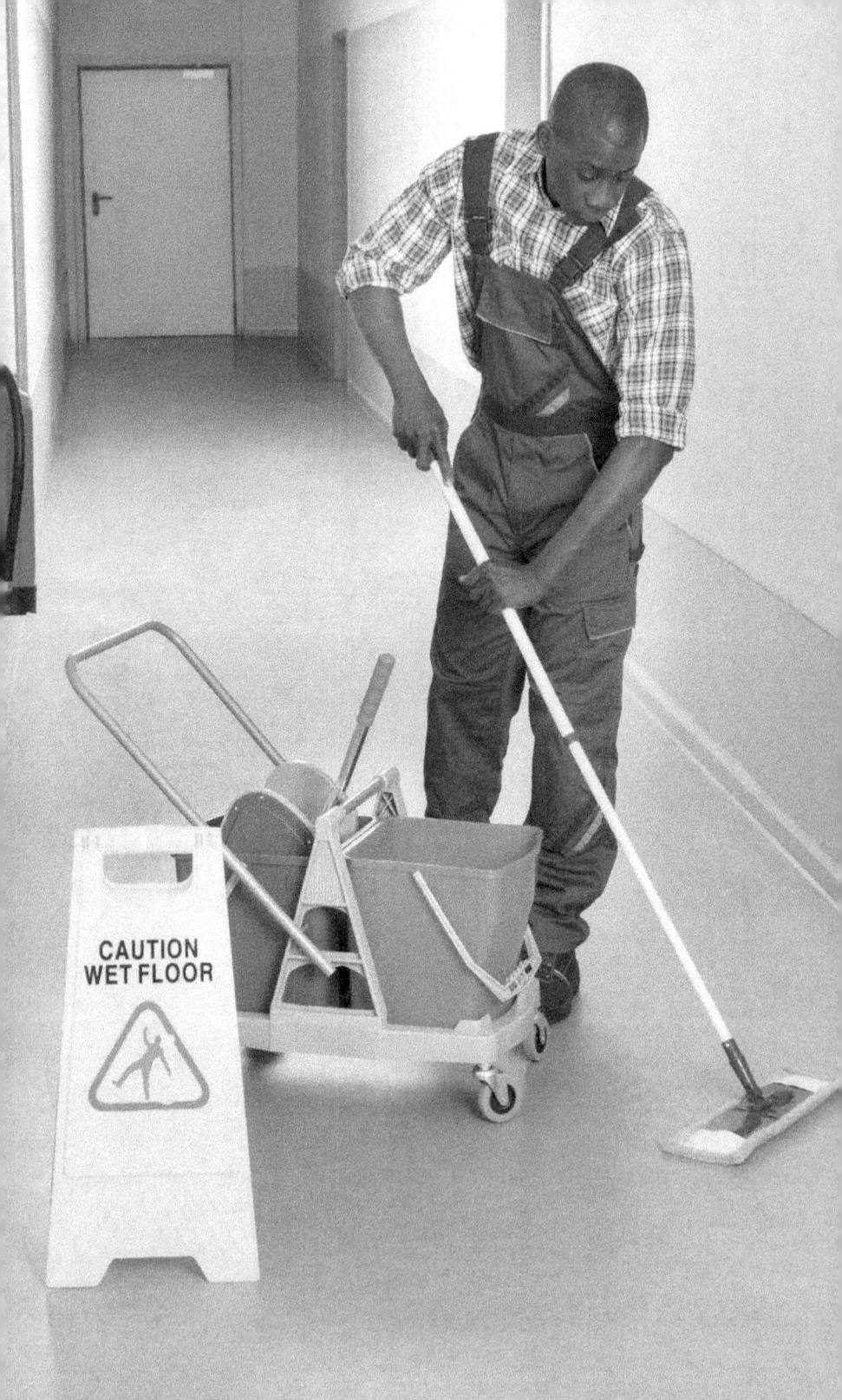

Survival Step Three

Keep your roadway clear

I have walked that long road to freedom. I have tried not to falter

NELSON MANDELA

BME NHS staff are a credit to the NHS and public services, yet we find ourselves disproportionately being the subject of disciplinary proceedings. The recognition that systemic factors, management and discriminatory practices has given rise to this situation has been clearly acknowledged. BME staff, like non-BME staff are of course legitimately face organisational proceedings and that must continue to be the case to safeguard the public, and staff. There is no question that BME staff working in the NHS must face lesser scrutiny and disciplinary processes, however they must not face these proceedings unjustifiably which is currently the case. The responsibility for this rests firmly with NHS organisations, and leaders.

It is now well known that BME NHS staff are more likely face disciplinary procedures than non-BME staff. Leadership in NHS organisations must commit to taking action to improve this situation, and the introduction of the **Workforce Race Equality Standard** (WRES) into the NHS in April 2015, will focus attention on this. One of the WRES metrics is:

Relative likelihood of BME staff entering the formal disciplinary process, compared to that of White staff entering the formal disciplinary process, as measured by entry into a formal disciplinary investigation.

NHS Organisations are now expected to demonstrate progress against this metric over time. So as many factors are outside the control of BME workers, are there any protective factors or steps that can be taken? There may be an argument that BME NHS staff should not be asked to consider specific steps they can take, and that it is entirely for organisations and leadership to take measures to bring about change. But the argument here is that BME workers, even when excellent, are still at a disadvantage.

It is therefore a recommended survival measure to take steps to keep your roadway clear, and useful to know this at the start of an NHS career.

Recommended actions include:

1) Compassion checker
   People take jobs in the NHS for many reasons; it is unrealistic to expect that everyone was motivated by a calling or vocation. For many, it is a job, and there is nothing wrong with that. But everyone working in the NHS must remember that the primary purpose of their jobs is for the benefit of people who use the NHS services. It is necessary therefore to always act in ways that reflects this. For some this means adherence to a professional code of conduct, but mostly it is about treating people as you would wish to be treated.

2) Relationships
   Cultural, racial and ethnic backgrounds can be seen as barriers to achieving good relationships between some staff, but many diverse staff teams have positive experiences of working together. If you are from a BME background, and particularly if you have a strong cultural identity in the workplace, you may find some colleagues feel they don't or can't understand or communicate with you. Allegiances, cliques, friendship groups can easily form, with decisions made behind the backs of those that should be included. If you are from a BME background, some of these factors may be compounded for you and there are rules you will may need to play by:

a) Make sure there is an open forum where decisions are formally made, that you always attend, even if you feel frozen out.

b) Record-keeping/documentation - If you are concerned about decisions that you should be a key part of, ensure there is written evidence of your inclusion or omission in making the decision. Write an email asking for confirmation, or ensure clinical records, or decisions taken in meetings are documented and up to date. Also, make sure there are records of any discussions you have with your supervisor, documenting any concerns you have.

c) Informal communications - It is critical to get involved in the informal conversations in the workplace, and keep consistent with it. Success with this depends on others being willing to engage with you at this level, so focus on those that will engage so you can always demonstrate willingness.

d) Socialising - again, as with informal communications in the work settings, it is important to participate in some of the social activities that take place outside work. Some teams go out each week, others less frequently. To never join in may be seen as problematic, yet some teams organise events that only appeal to some members. Consider joining forces with another team member to organise a team event, something you know you will enjoy, and everyone else will also.

3) Performance

Achieving a good job performance is critical to survival as open to disciplinary action if management decides this is the case. Judgements about your performance will be subjective, so do what you can to make sure your job performance is of a consistently good standard. Linked to job performance are the essentials of a good record of attendance, a satisfactory sickness record where your health allows it, and timekeeping (arrival at work, and arrival at meetings).

This Survival Step isn't about never putting a foot wrong, because developing is about learning and growing from experience where you don't already have the expertise. BME staff have the right to do this learning in an equal way with all NHS staff.

Survival Step Four

Get connected

Whatever affects one directly, affects all indirectly. I can never be what I ought to be until you are what you ought to be. This is the interrelated structure of reality

MARTIN LUTHER KING, JR

The people you have around you, in your corner, supporting you are critical to your survival as a BME NHS worker. There are many opportunities for making good connections in the NHS and that is one of the key strengths of the service enjoyed by many. Sometimes opportunities to make and maintain helpful connections will be easy to find and develop, but if you are from a BME background, you may find that you have to work harder to ensure that support is in place.

The support you need comes from influential and helpful individuals who understand your needs and are willing to help you, and it also comes from groups and networks able to do the same. This section describes examples of individuals and groups, internal and external to the organisation you work for, that you can connect to, sometimes for the whole of your career.

Mentors

These are staff members who are more experienced than you, in your workplace, or external to it, who are interested in helping you develop and achieve your professional goals. They might be someone you identify that is further down a career path that you want to emulate, and are prepared to share their experience, wisdom, ideas and help you shape your career. If you are interested in working for your employer on a long term basis, then a successful mentor within your organisation might be a good idea. It will be up to you whether you choose a BME or non-BME mentor, but their skills as a mentor is paramount. Some senior BME staff, although successful may not be able to advise you on race equality aspects of your development, and some non-BME mentors may be able to offer skilled advice, dependent on their experience.

An internal mentor knows the organisational back story, individuals, and how things work. They should be someone who is well respected, involved, engaged, and able to challenge rather than accept the status quo, while getting results. An internal mentor may need to balance their commitment to mentoring you with balancing their own interests in the workplace, which might sometimes conflict. Some mentors only take on the responsibility to build their CVs and not because they are really interested in developing you as an individual, or in mentoring generally. They may not be particularly good at it.

An external mentor will give you an outside perspective of your organisation, one that is not blinkered by alliances, relationships, and self-interests. They may be disadvantaged by not knowing the organisation, but if they work for the NHS, they will have insights that can be shared from their own organisation due to how the similar the NHS is throughout.

Sponsors

There have recently been more attention has been given to the high value of sponsors in the workplace. Rather than just being focused on helping you to develop your career, a sponsor will actively advocate and promote you within the workplace, rooting to make sure real opportunities to come your way. Some of the most successful NHS senior staff have had sponsors interested in their careers who have gone out on a limb to secure them opportunities for promotion, helping to make it happen, helping them up each step of the ladder. Unlike mentors, sponsors are supporters within your workplace. Be clear on the **difference between mentors and sponsors** and make a plan of how to incorporate them into your career.

BME staff often are unaware of sponsorship because it is a grey area. The role of the sponsor is not officially recognised or identified in the NHS as it may expose inequalities in managerial behaviour towards junior staff. In fact, the actions of sponsors often plays a large role in fuelling race inequality in the NHS, as their decision about who to sponsor can leave BME staff out in the cold. However, if fairly and formally organised and operated, it can be a positive tool for promoting all staff. The question may arise about whether a sponsor can in reality actively advocate and promote all staff they manage. Potentially not, as if a promotional opportunity emerges, a line manager will be duty bound to inform all eligible junior staff equally. Frequently this does not happen, and BME staff may find they are the last to know about forthcoming opportunities in their work settings, and therefore be less prepared.

A sponsor therefore is unlikely to be your direct line manager, but someone senior, with more of a helicopter view of emerging opportunities, inside your organisation but also external opportunities. They are likely to be very effective networkers, be influential, and an opinion-former. People seek their views and recommendations.

So how do you find a sponsor? You are most likely to meet them through networking, when you present yourself in a position to impress them. Perhaps you may meet them at a conference when you are speaking, or running a workshop, or launching your book, or published paper or article. They will need to view you as an interesting person, with potential, and you will need to make it clear to them you are seeking opportunities. You will need to click with your prospective sponsor, you will need to like each other and get on well.

Exchange contact details, and arrange to meet up every now and then. Be explicit about your dreams and goals, and show them that as well as being aspirant, and ambitious you are also a self-starter. You will not be relying on them to do any heavy lifting. If they become aware of an opportunity in the future, they want to be able to quickly give you a contact name, website, email address and expect you to take it from there. They will lead you to the water, but you definitely have to drink it yourself. Remember that at times they may be putting their own name and reputation on the line, and they need to have confidence in you before recommending you.

Networking

There are different types of networks internal and external to your place of work which you will be able to use to find supporters, build your reputation and credibility, and increase your visibility. They may be research, educational, or academic networks, and although are more likely to be available to clinical professionals, they can also exist to promote good practice in workers in all roles in the NHS. Leading busy lives, NHS workers are benefiting from a number of e-networks such as the **We communities**, and the **Guardian Healthcare Professionals Network**.

BME networks

This is the opportunity provided by employers to form a forum for BME workers to meet exclusively to discuss specific issues affecting their experience in the workplace, from a BME perspective, and to provide a supportive space to freely air issues. These forums usually feed into the workforce and organisational development directorate and can bring issues to the attention of the organisational leadership and effect change.

There is a **national NHS BME network**, not exclusive to NHS staff as the discrimination and marginalisation

59

experienced by BME NHS staff is often mirrored in the experience of BME patients and carers using the NHS. **NHS England** has its BME staff network and may be a good starting place in identifying an approach.

Non-NHS BME networks

There are a number of leading think tanks, campaigning and policy groups such as the **Race Equality Foundation**, and the **Runnymede Trust** that seek to raise awareness of race inequality in the NHS and secure improvement actions.

Making the right connections can not only serve you well for career development, but can be vital alliances during challenging times, for the provision of advice, information and support.

Activism

NHS BME staff are increasingly aware that their experience is part of a wider social, historical and political narrative that has led to the global oppression by non-BME people. Their problems in the workplace have been framed within a workforce and organisational context but when the walls of the institution are removed, race discrimination in the NHS is simply part of the continuum of wider rights breaches. As such, they become part of the wider fight for social justice and question can be asked about how long it will be before this fight is taken outside the walls of meeting rooms, grievance hearings, board meetings, conferences, and universities where they have been scrutinised for decades without improvement, and in fact with the problem worsening.

We just need to look at the campaigns that staff have taken to the streets about over recent years – junior doctors contracts, staff pay, nurses' bursaries etc. have all seen staff march through the streets, take industrial and strike action, lobby Parliament and even take their case to the high court. Not the issue of a proven catalogue of injustices towards BME staff. Why is this? Why are the trade unions not taking this up as a leading campaign and calling for a ballot unless there is improvement? Why are BME staff not organising to take militant action? There is a large body of activists with the potential to support them, but their story is poorly known and there is widespread laissez-faire about the situation.

Calls to action are starting to be heard however, for example Lee Jasper's Campaign NoWREStilequal which provides a stinging critique of the WRES initiative, and speech and the work of the Black Health Forum in Bradford. Other campaigns that focus on race equality, and challenging systems, relevant to this debate, include:

- Black Lives Matter UK
- Reparations UK
- Save Our NHS
- Occupy Movement

The question can be raised whether the reason this situation has not improved, but has worsened over the decades is because it has been contained, silenced and disempowered within institutions. Had it taken to the streets, been brought to the public's attention, and been fought (non-violently) on the streets, there would have been rapid progress towards equality, fairness and justice by now.

Survival Step Five

Know and stand up for your rights

No change can come if those who are impacted the most by discrimination are not willing to stand up for themselves.

ZAINAB SALBI

A key step in survival is to know your rights in the workplace: your entitlements as a BME worker in the NHS. These are the same rights and entitlements for everyone working in the NHS, however lack of awareness can prevent BME workers from speaking out or taking self-protective action. In previous steps in this series, I wrote about setting up your line of defence from the start of your NHS career (Step 1), to understand your obligations to your career and to others (Step 3), and knowing your rights completes the triad for the firm foundations to survive, and enjoy a career in the NHS as a BME worker.

The main rights you will need to be aware of are employment rights set out in law; organisational policies, often based on law, professional codes, and those rights set out in the NHS Constitution. This is knowledge you are recommended to be aware of, understand, without a need to draw on this on a day to day basis. It is not necessary to carry these rights around with you waiting for something to go wrong. Knowing your rights doesn't mean you are more likely to use that knowledge, and seek to assert your rights inappropriately. In fact most organisations have processes in place to prevent the exertion of rights when it is not required, or if used maliciously. Your main rights in the workplace, some of which are covered by legislation are to:

- A fair pay and contract framework;
- Right to be involved and represented in the workplace;
- A healthy and safe working conditions and an environment free from harassment, bullying or violence;
- Treatment that is fair, equal and free from discrimination
- Take a complaint about their employer to an

Employment Tribunal in certain cases

- In addition, the NHS, through its Constitution has made a number of pledges to staff:

- A positive working environment for staff

- Clear roles and responsibilities and rewarding jobs

- Personal development and education and training

- Support with health, wellbeing and safety

- Opportunities to be involved in decisions that directly affect them

To encourage and support staff to raise any concern with their employer in the public interest

The performance of the NHS on race equality for BME workers has been shown to be poor over many indicators, and getting worse. This tells us that laws and pledges mean nothing if they are not making a difference and bringing about change. Action that is needed must be that which effects change, or it is not worth the time and effort.

There is a laisez-faire tolerance of sub-threshold racism that BME staff put up with, and leaders turn a blind eye to. Without a zero tolerance approach to race inequality against BME staff in the NHS, the position will remain static.

Many initiatives such as BME leadership programmes, and the Equality Delivery System, have been developed and run with limited effect on the bigger picture. Now for the first time, the requirement to report and demonstrate progress against a Workforce Race Equality Standard has been written into the NHS contract in 2015, and will be monitored thereafter.

This will be the first real test for the NHS in whether it can deliver its own self defined standards on achieving race equality.

Knowing your rights is important, but more important is standing up for your rights. Breaches of policies, organisational values, codes of conduct, and the law may sometimes be difficult to prove, but many of these matters are conducted blatantly. The reason for blatant infringes of legal or NHS standards is a culture of arrogance, cronyism, and a sense of certainty that things will go unchallenged.

BME colleagues complain regularly to each other, and supporters, of infringes of practice, standards and codes with themselves or others being on the receiving end. But they feel too isolated or too intimidated to do anything about it. Many people choose to do nothing. I have chosen to do nothing, and walk away in the past. If we all walk away, without taking action, this behaviour will never be checked.

Don't doubt yourself, your instincts or your entitlement to fairness and equality. Find the strength, and support to make a complaint, or bring a case. People choosing to walk away from bullying and harassment, and move into another job, or move into temporary roles such as agency nursing or interim contract working is not a solution. This only emboldens people who exhibit such behaviours to continue, and driving BME staff out of their good jobs, or preventing them from gaining promotion, can become an objective of a culture of bullying and harassment.

I have had just cause to successfully bring a grievance which was upheld and resulted in disciplinary action against the line manager. Had I not taken the action I had, I would not be in the senior NHS role as I am currently, but probably working in a low graded temporary position, possibly outside the NHS. Working in a culture where one is experiencing bullying and harassment is harmful to health, because of the impact of stress. Stress can induce a range of physical health problems that can have very harmful damage to health.

Survival Step Six:

Influence your leaders

Good leadership is key to the success of any organisation. Any organisation must always appoint the best leaders and in NHS if we don't, patients, staff and the NHS will suffer. They set the tone, language and culture of the organisation Sadly NHS has club culture, Old Boy's network and hence it tends to appoint same old leaders and managers and this puts patients, staff and NHS at risk.

DR UMESH PRABHU (2017)

Leaders of NHS organisations have a duty of care towards staff employed to provide services. Survival Step Six is to understand how leadership operates, how to hold leaders to account, and ultimately how to become a good leader. There are many exemplary NHS leaders running the some of the best organisations in the country, with effective leadership at all levels. This is not the case throughout the NHS and this impacts the experience of everyone working and using organisations. The NHS is structured on hierarchical basis, based on the army management systems, replicating power systems and culture.

Your line manager

This is the person you report to directly on a day to day basis and who represents management in the organisation. They may be a team leader, team manager, ward manager, charge nurse, ward sister, or supervisor. They typically manage team numbers of between six and thirty. Many staff may have little knowledge or contact with leaders in their organisation beyond their manager. Line managers wield a lot of power and authority, as those they manage are often the lower grades in the organisation. Those least likely to the have the broader knowledge and skills of how their organisation works. The more junior you are, the more likely you are to have a line manager, with those at the top of the hierarchy.

Staff can have the most positive, fulfilling and enhancing relationships with their line managers, but that can be down to luck. The experience for too many is a line manager who is a poorly equipped for the job, with knowledge and understanding of management. Worse, they may also lack the personal qualities such as honesty, fairness, integrity and trustworthiness. They may draw on the worst human qualities to deliver leadership outcomes including bullying, intimidation, manipulation, deceit and aggression.

The reason for the common existence of line managers with poor values and skills are these characteristics are very commonly held by many NHS staff and the there are inadequate selection procedures to ensure these are eliminated from the service. In many cases, the opposite happens and staff known to possess these undesirable qualities is frequently promoted to leadership positions. So, if these qualities are so undesirable, why do these people get promoted? The simple reason is that the people promoting them possess the same qualities and find it acceptable to appoint others like themselves.

There are many rungs of line management, and you will probably be aware of who manages your line manager – and that may be as far as it goes. Staff in these posts remain for a few months to several years.

Service manager

At this level, the manager is usually responsible for a number of teams, clinics or service areas and is charged with ensuring the operational functioning of the service. They will have a number of managers that they manage who are responsible for operations at a lower level. The service manager does not usually get involved in day to day operational management as that is left to the team managers, who will then escalate issues that they cannot deal with to the service manager. The service manager's role is also operational, but is also strategic and responsible for the vision and longer term planning for the service. They also act as direct line manager. They report to senior management levels in the organisation, providing assurance of the functioning of their service, managing risk, and providing improvement plans. Managers typically remain in these roles for two to five years.

Assistant Director/Director

Responsible for a large directorate or division, and reporting to a Director, Ads are responsible for operational and strategic service delivery, and devote a lot of time to senior level operations.

Directors and Executive Director

Directors work at sub-board level, with Executive Directors being Trust Board members, and being the most senior officer for their service area.

Professional Leaders

These staff are often given job titles such as 'Head of' or 'Lead' and provide clinical leadership for disciplines of staff such as Allied Health Professionals, Nurses, Psychologists etc.

Promotion in the NHS too often brings with it a sense of entitlement. A perverted sense of entitlement with senior positions being perceived as a 'reward' for previous years of service. There is, among some NHS leaders, a sense of escape, and removal from hard work and conditions of workers at more junior levels. Too many of those who have 'arrived' have the perspective that life for them should now be as easy, they will stand on the shoulders of others, breathing in clean air, and have an army of people to do the work, and report to them.

They fail to understand what 'assurance' means, believing erroneously that this is about receiving committee reports from those further down the ladder, and bringing pressure to bear on the juniors to report positive stories. Some Trust boards foster a culture where it is impossible to bring hard truths to board meetings, especially to the public part of the board.

Leading healthcare is tough, and things will go wrong. But too many boards see things going wrong as a personal threat to their power, status, and jobs and have great intolerance to hearing bad news. So their stance on bad news is to pretend they are not aware of it, or to not to want to be told about it, or they only want to hear about it once it has been sorted. The mantra is often 'don't bring me problems, bring me solutions'. But this approach absolves them from providing support, and taking responsibility. If leaders genuinely prioritise people over their jobs, their main concern should be to identify and root out risks, and problems, admit when things have gone wrong, and take action to correct them.

So what can you do to impact leadership as a survival step? Three actions are outlined:

1. Know and understand how leadership in your organisation works. Attend meetings that are part of your role. If they are not, ask to start attending and observing them as part of your development.

Attending the organisation's governing body meeting such as Trust Board meetings at least twice each year is a very useful part of your education, and provides an overview of roles. Other meetings that are useful to attend are quality, governance, audit, safety, performance and workforce development. These meetings are often provide opportunities to ask questions, and you should take the opportunity to do so.

2. Learn how to manage your leaders. Start by understanding the difference between managers and leaders. The NHS appears to be more committed to a management style of leadership, and for most of your career, you will report directly to a line manager. This is the person you will report to directly on a day to day basis, and the person you will rely on for your first line of support, information and guidance.

   Unfortunately, you will probably find that some line managers do not have appropriate managerial or leadership qualities, and may not even be interested in staff management. Managing staff may simply be an inconvenience that came with the promotion or grade they were interested in. Many see it as a cross they have to bear, and pay little attention to the needs of their staff team. In such cases you will need to decide if you can contribute and progress sufficiently with that manager, long enough to move on to another role, or whether it would be in your best interests to move on sooner. Explore whether you are able to take steps to bring out the desired managerial and leadership qualities in your line manager. It may be that they do not currently have the competencies, but do listen, and will develop and improve over time. In such situations, there will be benefit in staying in role, contributing and growing. However, with a poor manager, who has no insight, competencies, or the will to change and grow with their team, you will need to make a decision about your future with that manager. This is where mentors and particularly sponsors can be useful sounding boards.

3. Aspire to Leadership - If you are interested in leadership, take active steps to put yourself on this path. There is no rush, as arriving in senior posts that you are not appropriately skilled, experienced and prepared for, as that will prove to be a step too far, too soon.

    There are **BME leadership programmes** available, and it is a matter of personal choice if you want to pursue that avenue. The main benefits are opportunities to network and build alliances with other BME NHS staff that will provide useful sources of support during your career.

4. Learn from the best leaders: One of the most inspirational NHS leaders today is **Dr Umesh Prabhu**, Medical Director at **Wrightington, Wigan and Leigh NHS Foundation Trust,** a beacon NHS trust in equality standards in the NHS. Dr Prabhu, and his perspective on leadership brings many insights.

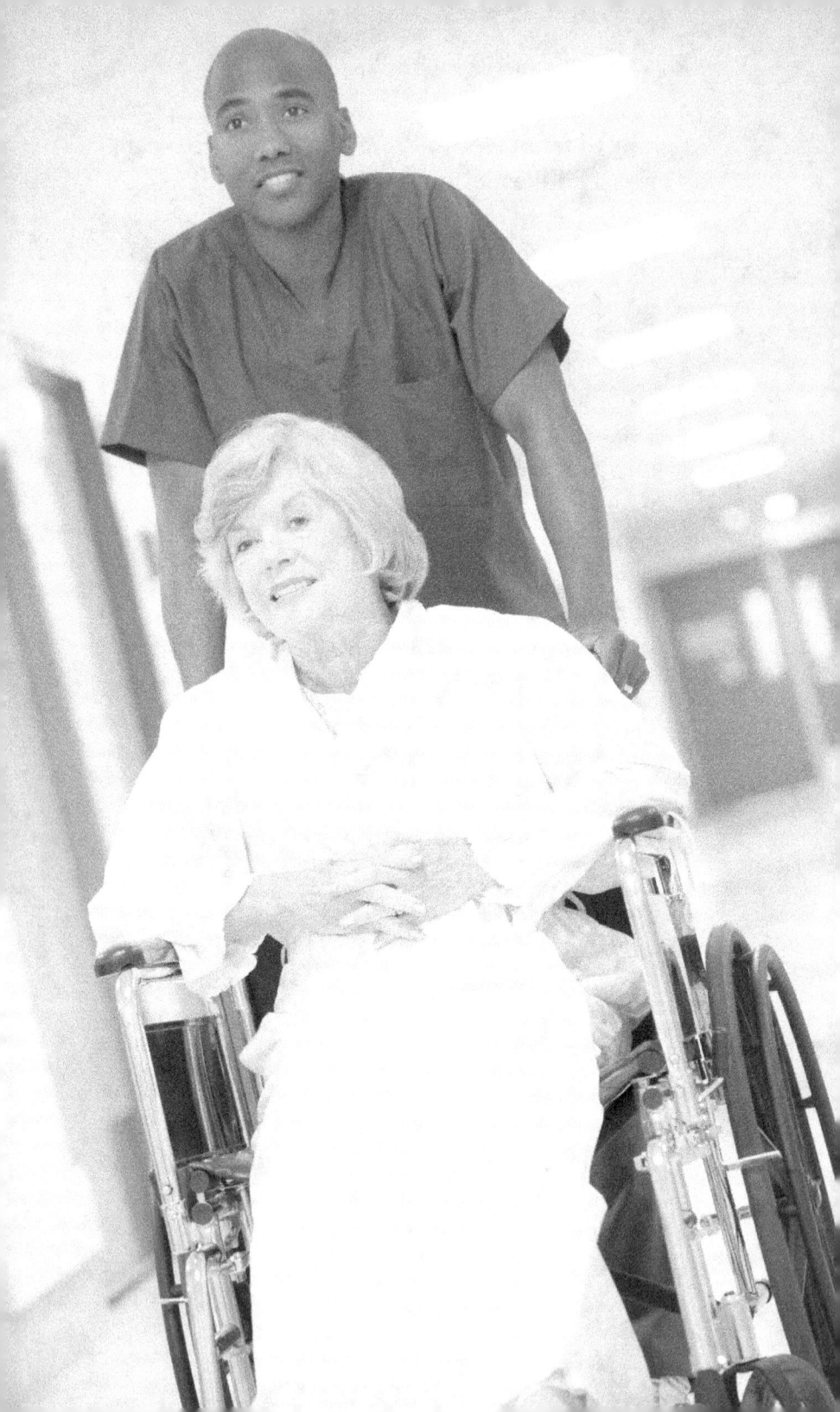

Survival Step Seven

Remain
Self-Empowered

*I have cherished the ideal of a
democratic and free society in which all
persons live together in harmony and
with equal opportunities.*

NELSON MANDELA

NHS BME staff face actions and experiences on a day
to day basis, in the course of their duty, that seek to
disempower them, or have the effect of disempower-
ing them. When staff have been promoted successfully, steps can be taken to undermine their seniority,
which can be demotivating.

The act of allocating senior BME staff to low skilled
duties and tasks, not commensurate with their grade,

is a covert way of undermining them, and belittling their abilities. This also amounts to demotion within grade.

This can happen because BME staff are often very experienced and skilled and because they have been under-promoted, and work with non-BME staff who have been over-promoted. This can cause a disparity, with BME juniors being more skilled and experienced than their non-BME managers which can cause tensions. The senior non-BME manager can seek to manage this by demotion within grade and giving demeaning work plan or holding back BME staff.

This can be seen in stark, and overtly racist behaviour, with an example experienced by the author within the last 10 years. Working as an agency nurse, in an office in a very prestigious private London hospital, I was sitting having a cup of tea with two non-BME nurses. We were all qualified, and enjoying the shift. Although I was an agency nurse, I was regularly booked to work there, as they knew me, and I fitted in well. On the day in question, we had called the on call doctor to carry out a non-emergency patient review. We three nurses were relaxed, enjoying our cups of tea when the doctor arrived on the floor. I didn't know him, but he appeared to know the other two who he greeted on entering the office. I smiled at him, as I do on greeting new people, but he didn't greet me. He started discussing the patient he was due to review, and talking to one of the nurses who was responsible for the patient in question. He then suddenly looked straight at me:

"Get me a cup of coffee" he ordered.

I was shocked, I didn't recall ever receiving such an order from a colleague ever before.

"Pardon?" I said

"Coffee. Get me a cup of coffee" He barked this order at me.

The other two nurses had taken in what was going on, but busied themselves about the office with patient notes.

The system for making hot drinks was very easy in this private hospital. There was a small kitchen area, well laid out with pretty cups and mugs, coffees, hot chocolate and a large range of herbal and fruit teas. Hot water, and milk were on tap, and everything set up so that catering staff, or nursing staff could quickly get a hot drink to the private patients instantly they demanded it. Staff were permitted to use this area for their own beverages and we helped ourselves throughout the shift, making quick drinks for ourselves and each other.

When this doctor so impudently repeated his question, I knew exactly what he was doing. He was smirking.

"If you go out of the office, just a few feet ahead you will see the beverage bay and you'll be able to help yourself to a drink"

With that I left the office to see my patients. I felt hurt, embarrassed and humiliated. But empowered also. There was no way I was going to make him a drink with that sort of demand.

Staff working on a ward work almost as a family. Very closely. Particularly in permanent teams. We help each other. No one orders someone to make them a drink in that manner. I knew there was no way he would order the two non-BME nurses on shift with me.

After I had finished my round, and attended to all my duties, the doctor had left the floor, and in the office once again with my two nurse colleagues neither of them referred to the incident. Not then, or ever. They didn't check to see if I was alright, or wanted to discuss the incident. Could they really have failed to observe what had happened? As with many similar incidents, my non-BME colleagues turned a blind eye to racist behaviour, as they considered it nothing to do with them.

NHS BME staff can find themselves disempowered through failure to attribute their good work and achievements to them, so that others, normally seniors take up your ideas and work and claim it as theirs.

NHS BME staff also experience failure to praise them

for their achievements and good work and achievements, and low thresholds for criticising their work.

There are several approaches to dealing with these issues, and according to context, and organisational culture, the general recommended approach is confidence, networks, support, with the emphasis being on having collective backing where possible.

Remaining empowered is about keeping the information from Steps 1 to 6 on board, so you draw on them periodically to power your development, and protect you from some pitfalls and provide support, information and guidance when needed.

More and more people are finding working in the NHS a game of survival, due to the scale of pressures on staff at all levels. There are many casualties, and many people experience discrimination and poor treatment because of poor leadership and organisational culture.

Survival Step 7 suggests taking stock through a Seven - Step Checker, a checklist that you can complete periodically, to keep you aligned to the Seven Steps. BME NHS staff are recommended to take steps to develop their own personal survival checklist, but examples are set out here:

Checklist questions

Step 1. Line up your defence
Checker: Are my union and/or professional membership subscriptions up to date?
Step 2. Write a new script and commit to a higher level of engagement
Checker: How many reports or publications on my area of NHS work have I read in the past 3 months?
Step 3. Keep your roadway clear
Checker: Are there any work relationships that need attention or input?
Step 4. Get connected
Checker: Do I have/need a mentor or sponsor? Have I explored union membership? Checker: Have I joined any relevant networks and what progress is that achieving?
Step 5. Know your rights and obligations
Checker: Are there any relevant policy areas that need updating, any policies I need to read?
Step 6. Influence your leaders
Checker: What is my relationship with my line manager? Is there any development work to do there? Checker: How many relevant meetings have I attended? Checker: Is leadership for me?
Step 7: Remain empowered

Checker: Assess your self-confidence levels, attend assertiveness training courses

This Seven-Step Checker can be tailored to meet individual needs, and it can become a part of your meetings with your line manager, your sponsor, your mentor, and be part of your annual appraisal, and your network discussions. It can be of useful toolkit for workforce and organisational development leaders, and NHS leaders. But it is intended as part of a toolkit for BME NHS worker's survival.

Last word – your new contract with the NHS

Earlier in the book, I outlined the historical context and the legacy of colonial and post-colonialism on the current race dynamics at play in the NHS. I described a contract, unwritten, but a contract nonetheless setting out the expectation of the contribution NHS staff would make during the post war era. This would be a transient, low-skilled contribution with an emphasis on the donation of labour in return for short term reward, giving rise to no entitlements other than pay for work done. Although the contract has been extended, in many cases through several generations, so has this contract of limited scope. It is now time to write your new contract with the NHS, setting out the full scope.

Do this through confident, positive affirmations, writing uplifting statements or quotes that you use to steer you every day until you reach your goal. Affirmations are personal, but here are a few thoughts to steer by;

- ✓ I have the right to enjoy all the benefits of my job

- ✓ No one is better than me, and I am better than no-one

- ✓ Each day I take a step to move further into my destiny

- ✓ I am not submerged by events, I learn from adversity every day

- ✓ I share my burdens with others, and help others in theirs

- ✓ I enjoy a 'win' at work everyday

About the Author

Claudia Tomlinson is a senior manager in the NHS, having worked in the service over many years. She has delivered a wide range of roles in mental health care, operational, strategic and project management. An activist, a successful blogger, coach, public speaker, and social media commentator, she is also author of "Revalidation for Nurses and Midwives – A Handbook for Registrants".

www.ingramcontent.com/pod-product-compliance
Lightning Source LLC
Chambersburg PA
CBHW071223280526
45787CB00002B/782